THE DELUSION OF UNBELIEF IN A SCIENTIFIC AGE

HOWARD TAYLOR

THE HANDSEL PRESS

Published by
The Handsel Press Ltd.
33 Montgomery Street, Edinburgh

ISBN 0 905312 69 4

Printed by
W. M. Bett Ltd, Tillicoultry

ACKNOWLEDGEMENTS

It was Professor T. F. Torrance whose lectures inspired me to try to get to grips with relativity and quantum theory. I also express my gratitude to him for reading and commenting on my original draft. His correctives have deepened even further my understanding of the essential openness of the universe. I am also very grateful to Dr Martyn Cundy for his very helpful comments and corrections especially in relation to Gödel's Theorem. However, the imperfections of this little book are entirely my responsibility.

I am greatly indebted to Mrs Iona McFarlane of Innellan and Miss Isabel Gardner of Glasgow for labouring with my appalling hand writing to type the manuscript. Very sincere thanks too, to Tony and Agnes Miles of Innellan for their generosity in putting their Word Processor at my service.

HOWARD TAYLOR

Spring 1987

INTRODUCTION

Twentieth century western man is in the grips of a delusion of unbelief. He has wanted to explain the existence of the universe, the laws of nature and of life itself, without any reference to God. If he can push God out of his origins, he can push Him out of his daily life too. However, the thought that all of nature can be explained from within itself always has been a nonsense. The further science advances into the nature of reality the clearer it becomes that we depend for our very being on the grace of God.

Albert Einstein implied that it was the greatest scientific minds who were aware of a religious dimension to reality. I believe this is because a humble awareness of God actually liberates the mind to think. What he actually said was:

> 'You will hardly find one among the profounder sort of scientific minds without a religious feeling of his own.... His religious feeling takes the form of rapturous amazement at the harmony of natural law, which reveals an intelligence of such superiority that compared with it, all the scientific thinking and acting of human beings is an utterly insignificant reflection. This feeling is the guiding principle of his life and work, in so far as he succeeds in keeping himself from the shackles of selfish desire. It is beyond question closely akin to that which has possessed the religious geniuses of all ages.'
>
> (Quoted from John Polkinghorne in an article *The Faith of a Physicist*, published in *Physical Education* 22, [1987].)

Yet so many since Einstein have not wanted to admit it! Pride and prejudice against radically new ways of thinking involve us all as sinful human beings. Scientists are no exception to this. Sadly now, it would be a radical new departure for much of the scientific establishment to think of a Creator and Sustainer of the natural world. Even though the reality of God presses upon us everywhere in nature, we dare not face up to it. Two very eminent scientists, whom I shall be referring to in subsequent pages, are John Polkinghorne, Fellow of the Royal Society and now an Anglican Priest (a Christian), and Paul Davies, Professor of Theoretical Physics of The University of Newcastle (a non-Christian). They have recently written on the relationship between science and belief in God.

Both of them express the view that scientists are unique amongst human beings in being able to change their minds easily in the face of new evidence. John Polkinghorne, in his book *One World*, page seven, quotes approvingly words of Karl Popper as follows:

> 'Science is one of the very few human activities, perhaps the only one, in which errors are systematically criticized and fairly often, in time, corrected ... in other fields there is change but rarely progress.'

Paul Davies in his book *God and the New Physics* says on page eight:

> '... the scientific community as a group is always ready to adopt a new approach.'

Frankly, I doubt this very much. I would have thought the history of science shows scientists to be just as obstinate human beings as the rest of us. Radical changes do take place but not without a great deal of difficulty. Twentieth Century scientists may think they are different from scientists of earlier generations, but they are not.

Of course there are exceptions and history learns to thank these exceptions for the progress in knowledge. John Polkinghorne is one such scientist who is willing to come out in the open and declare his belief in God. Paul Davies is prepared in his book, referred to above, to reveal his own intellectual and spiritual struggles with this question. Time and time again he comes to the point of admitting the reality of God and then attempts desperately to wriggle back again into his scepticism, using the most fantastic theories to help him – theories which have no foundation in experimental or mathematical fact. Having wriggled back, he confesses that he has a sense of 'unease' in his scepticism.

One of the best examples of sheer obstinate unwillingness of scientists to accept radically new ways of thinking is the tenacious way so many hold on to the theory of evolution as a mechanistic or materialistic explanation for the origin of all the species of life. To let go of it would shake the foundations of the way 'enlightened' Twentieth Century Western man has come to view himself as a creature not answerable or accountable to any Creative Mind. I believe that, although there is such a thing as small scale evolution, the evidence against it being a mechanistic explanation for the origin of the different forms of life is very powerful indeed. One listens in vain for scientific arguments for it. Instead, one hears little but assertions that evolution did this or that in nature, adding this or that limb to a creature, and those who do not accept it are nothing but cranks. We really should not be intimidated by such assertions, but listen carefully to the actual arguments advanced. More of this in Chapter 3.

Some scientists say that if we admit there is a God, without whom we cannot fully understand the natural world, then science will be redundant. The opposite is the case. Knowledge of God actually liberates the mind to think and explore His creation.

If we keep telling ourselves an untruth (even if it is obviously untrue) then we eventually believe what is untrue. That is the nature of man, as propagandists, and mind manipulators know. Intellectuals and academics are no exception.

In spite of all the unbelief that bombards us so effectively through T.V.

and the education system, the majority of ordinary people do think there may be a God. (Between 70%-80% according to recent surveys.) However, spiritual and intellectual weakness of some of the church's bishops and clergy who are much in public view, has meant that the church has become easy prey for the secular humanist establishment. It has often merely accepted the false assumptions of an unbelieving media establishment and has left the general public in a sort of belief-unbelief limbo, as it has retreated into a merely socio-political 'gospel' which can do little to tackle the basic problems of our society. The general public's religious instincts are however still alive, but with no reasonable direction these instincts branch out into the demonic supernatural, which is evidenced by a glance round any high street bookshop.

The ordinary man realises that there is more to reality than meets the eye – that the reality of God presses in upon him everyday in the sheer wonder of nature and life itself. In one sense every man is a scientist, in that he observes nature. Jesus told His disciples to consider (think about) the flowers of the field. Do they not point to an amazing Mind? Of course they do. The more the professional botanist examines the flowers, the more, not less, wonder he finds. The more botany and biology advance, the more incredible the picture of life which emerges.

In the first Chapter we shall look at what the latter part of this century has had to tell us about the nature of the universe (cosmology); in Chapter 2 we will consider the nature of the very small (quantum theory) and in Chapter 3 the nature of life itself. I will try to show that in each case our discoveries bear witness to what is beyond nature. Chapter 4 considers the sceptical philosophies of recent times. But before I finish this introduction I want to make a few more points.

Firstly, what do we make of the 'god of the gaps'? In the old days it was considered that certain natural phenomena could be explained by man, but that there was a vast number of occurrences in nature for which man had no explanation. One of these was lightning and thunder. It was assumed that these phenomena could only be explained by reference to God. God was necessary to explain the gaps in human knowledge. However, as knowledge advanced, the gaps became smaller so that the need for God became progressively smaller. It was assumed that man's knowledge would soon become so great that the gaps would eventually disappear enabling man to understand the universe purely materially, there being no more need for the concept of God to explain the physical universe. In fact the very reverse has been the case – so much so – that some physicists are giving up a materialistic view of nature. The farther science has advanced in its understanding of nature, the more wonder – not less – has been found. In answering one question it has discovered many more unanswered questions – questions it had never even thought of before. The gaps in knowledge have not got smaller, but far greater than previous generations could have imagined. Scientists have had to retreat from a self confidence that soon all would be explained, to a humble awe which should lead them away from an old fashioned materialism.

We thought that after Benjamin Franklin had discovered that lightning was an electric current between the clouds and the earth, we had solved the problem of what lightning is. No need for God any more to explain lightning. After all, every school boy and girl knows that a build-up of cumulus clouds causes static electricity in the clouds, so great that the potential difference between the clouds and earth causes an electric current to flow, and that is lightning. Problem solved! Ah, but what is an electric current? Answer: An electric current is a flow of electrons. Ah, but what are electrons? Answer: Electrons are tiny things with negative charges that revolve round the nucleus of an atom. Wrong! Since our advance in knowledge in recent decades, we now know that electrons are not 'things' at all. That is to say, they do not have a complete set of physical properties that belong to things! They are not just scaled down snooker balls. As our knowledge of the very tiny world of electrons advances we come face to face with a mystery which takes us way beyond an old materialism into a ghostly world that seems to be hinged to another world beyond nature.

So we thought we knew what lightning is! I came across the following quotation that goes back to 1890. However, its message is still true today.

Examiner:	What is Electricity?
Candidate:	Oh, Sir, I'm sure that I have learnt what it is – I'm sure I did know – but I've forgotten.
Examiner:	How very unfortunate. Only two persons have ever known what Electricity is, the Author of Nature and yourself. Now one of the two has forgotten.

The extraordinary mystery of the very fabric of existence will be discussed more fully in Chapter 2.

In God's Kingdom scientists will never be out of work. The further their knowledge advances, the more wonder and beauty they will discover as nature unfolds its infinite beauty to mankind, to the glory of Him who loves all He has made and preserves.

However, I must make it clear that I am not saying that some things in nature have a natural explanation and other things a supernatural explanation. That would be a 'god of the gaps' theory in the wrong sense. God is the creator and source of all that is, and its sustainer. The whole universe of nature depends for its continuing being on the grace of God and therefore cannot be explained entirely from within itself.

This really is the classical 'cosmological argument' for the existence of God. The very fact that the cosmos exists must mean that its existence depends on another beyond it. That is God, whose existence is not dependent upon another. That is to say, all natural existence is contingent. David Hume, the great 18th Century Scottish Philosopher, challenged this argument by saying if we postulate a God whose existence is not contingent, why not just say the universe is not contingent. But that is to apply a principle of the supernatural (its existence is not contingent) to the realm of nature. This cannot be done. I will refer to this again in Chapter 4. I believe Mathematics come to our aid at this point, in the form of Gödel's theorem.

In my opinion, Gödel's theorem is very relevant to the cosmological argument. Russell and Whitehead (two great philosophers and mathematicians of this century) had tried to build up a self-explanatory system of Mathematics based on pure logic. They failed, and Gödel showed that their effort was pointless from the beginning. His theorem proved that any system which is complicated enough to contain the whole number system always contains propositions which cannot be verified from within that system. Gödel himself realised that his theorem had metaphysical implications and it is now often quoted in writings about the relationship between science and belief. John Polkinghorne (in *One World* page 25) professes himself surprised by the result of Gödel's theorem. I don't believe we should be surprised. It seems to me to prove what should be obvious, that the full understanding of any system cannot come merely from within that system. Applying it to the system of the universe as a whole, one concludes that the universe of nature cannot be a closed self-existent, self-explanatory system. It must be open to something beyond nature. This is the result that physicists and biologists are also coming to as their studies advance.

However, the study of nature itself does not lead one directly to God. I am not proposing a form of natural theology. Paul Davies is surely wrong when in *God and the New Physics*, page IX, he says, 'Science offers a surer path to God than religion'.

What nature does, with all its wonders, is to compel us to seek for God. Indeed, whether we are mere casual observers of nature or professional scientists, it leaves us without excuse if we choose not to seek Him. But the way of knowing God is not with the tools of natural science. The way of knowing God is of humble prayer, repentance and faith, as we listen for His Word. It will be a Word about His own glory and His suffering for us, and our sinfulness. It will be a liberating Word that gives us new life and hope and it is the same Word which upholds the whole universe. To quote E. J. Ambrose (Emeritus Professor of Cell Biology in London University) – *The Nature and Origin of the Biological World*, page 168 – 'Simple faith will open to us a door into another universe, a new dimension for living'. Again on page 170 he says, 'This is a matter of faith, some would say blind faith. Could it be that it is an absence of faith which is blind?' That is the question I want to explore further in this little book.

1. WHAT IS THE UNIVERSE?

*'In the beginning God created the heavens and the earth ... and God said let there be light and there was light'. (*Genesis 1 v 2*)*

*'You Lord have your being from before the beginning of time'. (*Psalm 93 v 2*)*

It belongs to Christian belief that; (i) not only matter but also space (the heavens) and time owe their existence to God, who transcends mere time and space as we know them; (ii) the universe has not always existed but had a definite beginning; (iii) from God's first creation of light He began to work out His creative purposes for the formation of the universe of matter, life and human beings. Let us consider these points from the perspective of modern science.

(i) *Space and Time* – The ordinary view of space is that infinite space is an eternal container of various objects such as galaxies, stars and planets, which have found their places and motions within it. Similarly, time is regarded as an infinite line in which various events have taken place. That is to say that space and time are regarded as absolutes and not things at all. Space and time are seen, not as part of nature, but merely infinite containers in which nature finds its place. This was certainly the view of Isaac Newton and this view of space and time is the foundation of what is often called Newtonian physics. It runs counter to the Christian cosmology that thinks of space and time as themselves dependent upon God and therefore themselves part of nature.

It was Albert Einstein with his theories of relativity that brought the scientific world into greater harmony with the Judaic-Christian cosmology when he formulated the belief that time is not an absolute. There is no such thing as a universal 'now' which applies to all existence. When objects are moving very rapidly, relative to one another, with speeds approaching the speed of light, their time frames are entirely different. So in theory (though not yet in practice) if astronauts could be sent into space and travel around at these very high speeds they could return to earth after a time which to them would only be a few years (say) but find that the earth had aged hundreds of years, generations having come and gone. This 'special' theory of relativity is based on the theory and observation that light is a more fundamental constituent of the universe than even time, so that the speed of a beam of light will seem the same for any observer, however fast he is moving.

Einstein's 'general' theory of relativity goes a step further using the known properties of light, and relates space to mass, so that a large mass bends space. The curvature of space around a large mass is what constitutes that mysterious force which we all know about, but cannot fully understand, namely gravity.

So, to conclude, modern science, in line with classic Christian cosmology, based on the Bible, sees space and time not as containers in which nature has its place, but as part of nature itself and therefore part of the subject matter of scientific investigation.

(ii) *The Beginning* – Several decades ago the great debate among cosmologists was whether or not the universe had a beginning. Those who believed in 'continuous creation' believed that the universe was infinite and had always existed. Others claimed that it had a beginning in a so called 'big bang' of light and energy. Hubble's discovery that the further away from us an object is (e.g. a galaxy) the faster it is rushing away from us, implied an exploding universe that had once been much more tightly compacted together. It was then possible to calculate that approximately 15,000 million years ago it was all together in a tiny singularity of incredible density and temperature. This explosion of light/energy, seemingly out of nothing, was the 'big bang'. From this big bang of light/energy the galaxies, stars and planets eventually condensed. It was theoretically predicted that if such a big bang did in fact occur there should be an echo of it today in space in the form of low temperature background radiation. This radiation was indeed discovered by two scientists working for the American Bell Telephone Company.

The theory that the universe did begin in a big bang of light and energy is today the universally accepted theory of the origin of our universe, although it has many variations. The mere fact that the universe did begin, immediately poses the metaphysical question – who or what caused it to come into existence? Because this question is about what is beyond nature, it cannot be answered by natural science. But that does not mean we cannot know the answer. The way of faith, humility, repentance and prayer will open to us knowledge of an Eternal reality. We do not have to be scientists to find the answer.

However, scientists who do not wish to take the step of faith, even though faced with the ultimate questions, will use all kinds of fantastic theories to try to avoid the question of God. Paul Davies, *God and the New Physics* pages 41-43, is an example of this. He envisages the possibility of our universe of space-time being a mere daughter universe of a more fundamental universe to which our universe owes its origin. Because we are imprisoned by our own space time, our investigations can never give us any knowledge of this parent universe. However, it does postulate a non theistic cause of our universe, though beyond our reach.

However, Paul Davies, just a few lines later, confesses that he has a 'feeling of unease' about this kind of theory. For not only is it pure speculation with, in principle, no way whatsoever of verification, it also only pushes the question of origins one stage back. One is still left with the question of why there are any universes at all. The wonderful thing about the Christian Gospel is that there is a way of knowing God. It is not by the processes of natural science but it is none the less a real way of knowing.

Before finishing this section I must refer to a more plausible theory that gets behind the 'big bang'. Some physicists believe that our expanding universe will one day, under the force of its own gravity, begin to contract until after many billions of years it will all come together again in one big immensely dense and hot singularity called the 'big crunch'. Some speculate that from the 'big crunch' it may bounce back into another 'big bang' and the whole story repeat itself. So on this theory the 'big bang' that began our universe was the result of the 'big crunch' which ended a previous universe. This cosmology envisages an oscillating series of expansions and contractions. Does it solve the problem of genesis? No it does not. Steven Weinberg, Nobel Prize Winner for Physics, discusses the oscillating universe in his book *The First Three Minutes*. In each big crunch-bang the ratio of one set of energy wave particles to another set gets larger. If the oscillating series has been infinite then this ratio would now have reached its peak. It clearly has not, so therefore the universe is not infinite and it must have had a beginning.

The most comprehensible and reasonable statement about the origin of the universe was written thousands of years ago:

> 'In the beginning God created the heavens and the earth ... and God said let there be light and there was light'.

(iii) *The Formation of the Universe* – If the 'big bang' is a mystery, then so is the formation of the stars, galaxies and clusters of galaxies. It is popularly believed that the explosion of light-energy quickly cooled, forming the sub-atomic particles that make up hydrogen and helium gases. Great clouds of hydrogen pulled themselves together under their own force of gravity until, with increasing temperature, great nuclear fires lit themselves and stars began to shine. But why didn't the gases just keep on expanding without forming stars, or conversely, why didn't the 'big bang' soon collapse in on itself again? Sir Bernard Lovell has calculated that if the rate of expansion had been less by only one part in a thousand billion, then the initial fireball would have collapsed in on itself before its constituents would have been able to form any of the stuff of the stars. Similarly if its expansion had been a very tiny bit greater, gravitation would not have been able to have held the gases so that the stars could not then have formed. So we are living in a very finely tuned universe indeed! Who gave it this fine tuning? If the reader wishes to read a more detailed account of the mystery of this fine tuning, there is a very interesting article in the magazine *Scientific American* – December 1986, page 50.

Paul Davies's calculations lead him to an even more finely tuned expansion. According to him the expansion rate is tuned to one part in a million billion, billion, billion, billion, billion, billion, or one part in 10^{60}! (page 179).

If this is an accidental fine tuning it would, he says, be like saying that a bullet fired in a random direction could accidentally hit a target one inch in size, positioned on the other side of the observable universe!

Even more mind boggling is the formation of hydrogen and helium from the 'big bang'. Hydrogen and helium were the constituents of the stars, yet their formation by mere chance processes is highly unlikely. According to Paul Davies, the 'big bang' would have produced black holes far more easily than these gases which it is said later made the stars. If the initial state of the 'big bang' were merely random, the chances of it eventually producing hydrogen and helium would be one part in $(30^{10})^{10}$.

There is clearly a tremendous amount of order in the universe. Even a single atom is very highly structured by physical laws. Where did this structure and order come from? The second law of thermodynamics is one of the most fundamental laws of physics. It tells us that order always degenerates into chaos. In a closed system (not open to an outside world beyond it) order cannot generate itself. It is another way of saying that by themselves things will wear out, not improve. It is easy for an egg to break, but it cannot put itself together again. Humpty Dumpty is the second law of thermodynamics in Nursery Rhyme form! Even if a system is open to outside influences, it will not normally increase in order. Usually it will deteriorate. A whirlwind applied to pieces of a television set will not reassemble them. On the contrary, it will tend to break them up even further. Will the sun's energy, pouring on to the earth, produce the tremendous variety of life on earth? I do not think this possible. As we will see in Chapter 3, the incredible complexity of the very simplest form of life can hardly owe its origin to the sun's rays.

However, we have to note recent research in *far from equilibrium conditions* by Ilya Prigogine (Nobel Prize Winner for Chemistry). A fluid is said to be in a far from equilibrium condition when it is in such an unstable condition (due, for example, to big temperature differences within it), that it is near to breaking point. Ilya Prigogine has shown that in such conditions it can take on new order when it is open to the outside world, with which it exchanges matter and energy. However, this does not violate the second law of thermodynamics because the local increase in order in the fluid will be more than compensated by an even larger decrease in order in the outside world.

So where did the order in the universe come from if there is no Reality beyond the universe and the universe is therefore a closed system? If the universe is, however, open to an Order beyond its order, then one can see how its structure can be generated and renewed in accordance with this 'Order'. This would need to be beyond nature and therefore not itself subject to the second law of thermodynamics. Surely this Order is none other than the Logos or Word of God, of whom the Scripture says that 'all things were made through Him' and in Him 'was life, and the life was the light of men'.

There are some scientists who explain the wonderful order of life on earth, by saying that life on earth is only a temporary local increase in order in this part of the universe. But not only has the incredible complexity and beauty of life exposed by modern biology and botany made this seem impossible, it still leaves one with the problem that the *whole* universe is very ordered. Life may be local to this part of the universe but order is spread throughout the universe. If it wasn't there would be no universe of any kind at all. I will explain in the next Chapter why nothing can exist without order.

This is a very important point. David Hume, the famous Scottish philosopher, tries to counter the argument that because the universe seems designed it must have a Designer. He says that *any* universe would appear to be designed. He therefore concludes that *this* universe does not prove there is a Designer. In fact the reverse follows. It is true that *any* universe would appear to be designed, but this is only because any universe with any order at all (there can be no existence without order) *would have been designed, by a Designer*. I will refer to this in more detail in the final chapter. (Actually I prefer not to use the words 'Designer' and 'designed' of God and His universe. I would rather say that the universe depends for its origin and continuing existence upon His Creative Mind and Consciousness. However, the principle of my argument with David Hume remains the same.)

The universe is only comprehensible because it is ordered. When Einstein said that the only incomprehensible thing about the universe is that it is comprehensible, he was meaning that there is no way of knowing from within nature where the order in nature came from.

One more point before we leave this section. We all tend to be overawed by the sheer size of our universe. We seem so tiny in comparison with the vast universe. What is the point of it all?

Firstly, contrary to much modern thinking, the awesome size of the universe is not a recent discovery. Medieval thinkers may have believed that the universe was only small, but over 3,000 years ago someone wrote:

> 'When I consider your heavens, the work of your fingers, the moon and the stars, which you have set in place, what is man that you are mindful of him, or the son of man that you care for him?' (*Psalm* 8 v 3 & 4)

The writer goes on to say that the significance of man is not his size but the position of authority that God has given him. I believe that authority over nature is far greater than we have ever imagined, but I will expand on this later.

Secondly, many cosmologists are now saying that the universe had to be as large and as old as it is to produce the elements necessary for the make up of planet earth.

Elements such as iron did not exist in the early universe. They are produced, it is said, by giant supernova explosions of stars nearing the end of their lives. Thus, according to this view, the universe had to be old enough for large stars to burn out before the elements necessary for the formation of planet earth could be formed.

It would, they say, also have had to be large and old to give time for life to evolve as far as man. I do not accept this so called 'anthropic principle' because it assumes that evolution is necessary to explain the origin of man. However, it is worth noting that orthodox science is saying that the existence of man depended upon a large and old universe.

Thirdly, although man is very tiny indeed when compared with the galaxies, he is very large indeed when compared with the sub-atomic particles from which everything is made. In fact man, as far as size goes, seems to be neatly in between the sub-atomic particles and the galaxies. He varies in size from each by a factor near to 10^{15}.

But what are these sub-atomic particles and what is the reason for the natural laws of the universe? This is the subject of the next section and the subject opens for us even greater mysteries.

2. GOD, MAN AND THE LAWS OF NATURE

It belongs to the Judaic-Christian belief that:

1. God is the ground of the rationality of nature. The Laws of electricity, magnetism, gravity etc., which are fundamental to the behaviour of all created things, did not just happen to be what they are, but owe their origin to God. The foundation of these laws is the Logos or Word of God which expresses the Mind, Will, Grace and Love of God.
2. God is not only the Creator of all things but also their sustainer. The universe was not merely created and then left to continue in its own way independent of the Creator. Its continuing existence depends upon the grace of God; 'He upholds everything by the Word of His Power', say the Scriptures.
3. Although God is the creator and sustainer of all things, He has granted freedom to nature and especially to man. Man really is free. We do not live in a deterministic universe rigidly controlled by physical or Divine laws.
4. God gave to mankind the freedom and authority to rule the earth. Man's use of His freedom really does affect for good or bad the world of nature with which he comes in contact.

Let us consider these points in the light of modern science.

(i) *Reasons for the Laws of Nature* – School Physics, and to a lesser extent chemistry, introduce us to thinking about the reasons for the laws of nature. A metal (say) behaves as it does because of its molecular structure. But what is the reason for its molecular structure? We can answer that by considering the atoms which go to make up the molecules. But why do the atoms behave as they do? We can answer that by considering the electrons, protons and neutrons which go to make up the atom. But why do the protons, neutrons and electrons react with one another in the way they do? We can answer that by considering the quarks which make up the protons and neutrons and the various interconnecting wave particles. And so on and so on and so on, for ever? There are two alternatives.

Either firstly, if we never end in our search for a more and more fundamental structure of nature then we will never be able to find the reason for the laws of nature being as they are. Scientists will never be out of work but will ever be delving deeper and deeper into reality, getting nearer and nearer to an accurate description of nature, but never finally realising their goal.

Or secondly, what if scientists do find *the* most fundamental building blocks of nature and know there is nothing more fundamental to discover? Then they will not be able to explain the reasons for the properties of these fundamental building blocks, there being nothing more basic by which to explain them.

Thus, the reasons for the laws of nature cannot be found within nature itself. There must be an explanation beyond nature. As we saw in the introduction, Gödel's theorem in mathematics could lead us to the same conclusion.

Let us think of these two alternatives. How will we be able to guess that now at last we have reached the fundamental building blocks? If we discover phenomena which *in principle* have no natural explanation then we surely are at the boundary of nature and what lies behind the natural universe.

It seems to me that physics is approaching or perhaps has already reached the fundamental building blocks of matter and energy. This is because its discovery of the nature and property of such 'things' as electrons and photons (the fundamental wave/particles of light) in quantum theory, has led it into a ghostly world which seems to hinge into that which is beyond nature. Quantum physics is the study of the nature of the atom and the sub-atomic world.

Earlier I said that without structure or order nothing would exist at all. Someone might respond by saying that fundamental particles merely floating around would still be in existence. My answer to this is to say that fundamental particles are not 'things' at all. They only exist in relationship to one another. A relationship involves order and structure. Therefore structure and order are necessary for anything to exist at all. The second law of Thermodynamics tells us that order always degenerates. So where did order come from in the beginning?

There is a popular misconception about progress in quantum physics due to the excitement of many scientists about progress towards a unified field theory, which I will very briefly summarise here.

All matter is considered to be made from two families of fundamental wave particle, namely the quark family (from which protons and neutrons are made) and the lepton family (an electron is a type of lepton). Then it is believed that these wave particles relate to one another under the influence of three or four fields of force namely the strong, the weak, the electromagnetic and gravity. The strong force is mediated by 'gluons' and binds the quarks together. Any residue of the strong force keeps the protons and neutrons together in the atomic nucleus. The weak force is mediated by so called vector bosons and is responsible for radioactive decay. The electromagnetic force is mediated by photons (the quanta of light) and keeps the electron in 'orbit' round the atomic nucleus. Any residue of the electromagnetic force binds atoms together in molecules. The gravitational force is mediated by as yet undiscovered gravitons.

It is believed that these forces have a deeper unity than is yet apparent and it is hoped, by some, that soon they may all be inter-related in a 'unified field theory', which will be the basis for describing the unity of all the laws of nature. Professor T. F. Torrance believes that in principle a complete unified field theory will never be reached. This is because he believes the laws of nature are dependent upon an Order or Regulating Principle beyond nature and therefore cannot be completely defined and described within the bounds of natural science.

Also, although progress may give a more accurate *description* of reality, it will not begin to explain what these fundamental wave particles and forces *are* and why they are as they *are*. To describe something is not the same as explaining the reasons for its existence.

It is at these very fundamental levels of inquiry that the questions '*how* do things behave as they do?', and '*why* do things behave as they do?' converge into one question. One may try to describe how the fundamental forces of nature work but never be satisfied with one's efforts until one has dealt with the question, '*why* are they what they are and not something else?' This 'why' question is a question about purpose in nature and implies a Mind that gave it purpose. Professor T. F. Torrance has pointed out in a number of articles (e.g. *Fundamental Issues in Theology and Science*) that science has operated with a false dualism between these two questions which has led to a false separation between the natural and moral sciences.

When we do ask what *are* these wave particles and forces, we are led into a very strange world indeed.

Quantum physics takes us right away from our ordinary 'common sense' world of everyday experience. The popular school text book picture of an electron is a little sphere of negative charge revolving round the atomic nucleus. But, in fact, we cannot picture or describe the electron in terms of normal two or three dimensional diagrams. An electron has to turn twice before it presents the same face to an observer! In our normal common sense world, an object (such as a stone, a snooker ball or a planet) has a position and velocity. We can know both where it is and how fast it is going. In Quantum physics one cannot know both where an electron is and how fast it is moving. This is not because of imperfections in our measuring apparatus, but because of the very nature of an electron. If it has a position then its velocity is in principle unknowable. Thus an electron is not a 'thing' in the normal sense at all.

This ghostly, other worldly, description of an electron is the reason why scientists have always found it difficult to decide whether it is a particle or a wave motion. Sometimes electrons (and other sub-atomic quanta) behave as if they were particles and sometimes as if they were waves. Common sense would say they cannot be both. A wave is a movement which takes place in a medium. Thus there can be, for example, waves in the sea, the air and in pieces of elastic. The wave in the elastic is not a lump of elastic, but a *movement* in the elastic. If an electron is a wave, it is a wave or movement in what? Physicists say it is a wave of information. Fine, but in what medium is this information stored and from where did it come? So perhaps we should say it is not a wave but a particle. If it is a particle, it is a particle made of what?

Young's famous two slit experiment demonstrates that even a single seemingly isolated photon or electron seems to know that it is part of a wave motion. Thus a series of single photons or electrons, released from a source, seemingly isolated from their predecessor and successor, seem to know how to move in relationship to their predecessor or successor, so as to produce a wave pattern on a screen. This is a profound mystery.

Could it be that these sub-atomic wave particles are not isolated but bound together by some reality beyond our space time? The next section may shed a little more light on this question.

(ii) *Einstein, Podolsky and Rosen (E.P.R.)* – In 1935 these three great scientists wrote a paper in which they demonstrated that quantum theory predicts that if two photons (or other 'fundamental' wave particles) are released by a common source, then the result of a measurement on one of them will depend on the result of the measurement on the other, even if they are separated by vast distances, and in nature there is no way in which they can 'communicate' with each other. This mysterious fact is often referred to as EPR. Experiments using electron spin have verified this result.

Neils Bohr, one of the founders of quantum physics, asserted that it is not possible to regard the world as made up of separated bits. Until a measurement is made, both photons must be regarded as a single totality, even if separated by millions of miles. The relationship between these two wave particles cannot then have a natural explanation. A non-natural explanation is a supernatural explanation.

I quote Professor E. J. Ambrose's comment on EPR:

> 'Present ideas about atomic phenomena involve the concept that a 'ground swell' as it were, of information lies behind all phenomena we observe in the universe. When electrons or other particles suddenly emerge from this background of information, it is hardly surprising that they are still able to communicate in some way. ... That this ground swell of information should lie beneath the universe is surely what we should expect if Creative Intelligence is continuously at work in the universe, if as the theologians say, the Creator is immanent within His creation.
> (*The Nature and Origin of the Biological World* – p 181)

(iii) *Uncertainty and Freedom* – It seems that we do not live in a closed deterministic universe. The physics of Isaac Newton would assume that if only we know the position, property and the velocity of every part of nature, we could in principle predict everything that would happen in the future. This would mean that in principle Beethoven's music and Constable's paintings (say) would be predictable from the 'big bang'! There would be no freedom at all in nature, everything being inherently predictable. One wag has summarised the theory of evolution in terms of a definition of hydrogen gas (The major early constituent of the universe). 'Hydrogen is a colourless and odourless gas which given enough time turns into human beings.' (And presumably turns into wonderful works of music and art too.) Merely to state the deterministic view of the universe in these terms shows how absurd it is.

Heisenberg's Uncertaintly Principle is one of the landmarks of modern physics. I referred to it in section (i) of this chapter, though not by name. It is the principle that the position and velocity of a sub-atomic wave particle cannot be known at the same time. There is an inherent uncertainty and unpredictability in the fundamental structure of nature. Neils Bohr and quantum physics after him, have discovered that there are effects without causes in the quantum world. When we ordinary beings see something taking place we assume that it has a cause. Something happens because something else caused it to happen. Nothing happens without a cause. This seems common sense. Yet quantum physics says that events happen in the sub-atomic world which have no cause at all in nature – not that we haven't yet discovered the causes, but that natural causes do not exist. (see John Polkinghorne, page 10 and Paul Davies, page 102) If ever the study of nature cries out for an explanation beyond nature then surely quantum physics does! Albert Einstein resisted Neils Bohr's belief in the inherent uncertainty of the quantum world, because he thought it implied that there were irrational jumps in nature. This is what he meant by his famous statement 'God does not play dice with the universe'. We can agree with both Einstein and Bohr. Nature is not irrational, but its rational structure depends upon a Cause beyond itself.

This inherent uncertainty in nature does not mean chaos and randomness. There is structure in nature but it is a contingent structure. There is clearly a wonderful order and structure to all of nature. If there was not this order and structure, not only would science be impossible, but nothing would exist at all.

I believe that God has created and continues to preserve the world of nature in such a way as to give it order, not chaos, but at the same time freedom, not determinism. The universe is neither deterministic nor random. By His grace we exist in freedom. Without Him there would be no order (and therefore, as we have seen, no existence) and without Him there can be no freedom.

(iv) *The Freedom of Humanity* – One of the great mysteries of science and philosophy is the nature of human consciousness. Why am I me and not someone else? What does it mean to say I am me? In one sense the birth of an individual life (animal and human) is only one actual birth amidst a possible many million births. There are millions of individual sperms given by the male to the female for the fertilisation of her egg. Yet only one of them actually penetrates the female egg to produce a new baby. The others are all discarded and die. Does this mean that there was only one in a million chance that 'I' should exist? If it had been a different sperm from my father that had fertilised the egg would it have been me that was born or someone else? What is it that sees through my eyes, feels with my body and thinks with my brain? If my thinking is only the result of electrical and chemical processes within my physical brain, how is it I am aware of myself and you reader are aware of yourself?

Even David Hume, that great sceptic, who laid much of the foundations of modern materialistic scepticism, said about his thoughts on the philosophy of personal identity, 'I find myself in a labyrinth'. It is this awareness of ourselves (self-consciousness) that has led all peoples to believe in something that we often call the human soul or spirit. Modern behaviourists scoff at such notions. They say the whole of human reality is only physical and is all contained within the 3 dimensions of the human body. How shallow they are in their thinking! They ask where is the soul. Is it located inside the body, and if so, where? We should not be intimidated by such questions. Modern physics is on our side in at least two ways:

1. We know from the theories of relativity, as well as mathematics, that the whole of reality cannot be described as if it were contained in three dimensional space. Although we cannot imagine what is beyond our space-time in four, five or more dimensions, it is nonetheless real. Could it not be that the human soul belongs to these higher dimensions and hinges into our human brain in our space-time? Those many people who, near the point of death, have had beyond the body experiences, will enthusiastically agree with this.

2. We have already seen that the quantum world cries out for some explanation beyond our space time. What is even more intriguing is that our human consciousness even seems to affect this quantum world. Neils Bohr believed that the ghostly world of the sub-atomic wave particles only sharpens into reality when an observation is made. And (as Paul Davies says – page 103) 'You can decide what to look for. Look for its location and you get an atom at a place. Look for its motion and get an atom, with a speed. But you cannot have both'.

It would seem that our human consciousness has a bearing on the nature of the physical world. Paul Davies (page 135) says:

> 'On the one hand, the quantum theory endows the observer with a vital role in the nature of physical reality; as we have seen, many physicists claim that there is concrete experimental evidence against the notion of "objective reality". This appears to offer human beings a unique ability to influence the structure of the physical universe in a way that was undreamt of in Newton's day.'

This is a far cry from the downgrading of humanity by 20th century materialistic scepticism. Christian belief is that human beings were created by God as part of nature and yet uniquely created in the image of God, and given authority, freedom and responsibility to care for the earth. Human beings are the wonderful link between earth and heaven, heaven and earth. We should represent the love and holiness of God to all the earth and voice the praise of earth to heaven. God really has given us power and freedom over the earth. We really can affect it for good or evil. How tragic is human sin and our alienation from heaven! What tragic results it has for man and world! If quantum theory is right, it could mean that man's effect on nature is not just that he pollutes the earth with smoke and radiation, but that his influence on nature is far far deeper than he had ever imagined in the past. This point will be referred to in the last chapter.

It may be asked 'Was not the world violent and red in tooth and claw, before the advent of man?' For what these are worth I have two thoughts on this: (a) If the fall of man into sin affects nature then it affects space and time as well. Because we are imprisoned in our space-time we can never by our scientific efforts discover that paradise from which we fell. It lies beyond our space-time. (b) It is interesting to note, though very mind boggling indeed, that some physicists (e.g. John Wheeler quoted approvingly by Paul Davies, page 39) believe that the human observer not only affects the present but the remote past as well. This is so speculative that I wouldn't want to make anything of it - only to note it in passing!

I believe we human beings were given a wonderful and awesome destiny from which we have tragically fallen, through the misuse of our own freedom. This has affected our wonderful earth profoundly, for the worse, in ways which we cannot fully understand. Nevertheless, God has not given us up, nor has He forgotten His world. Through the death and resurrection of Christ, His work of new creation is begun for those who humbly trust Him. The whole of nature awaits the culmination of His purposes.

> 'The creation waits in eager expectation for the sons of God to be revealed ... then the creation itself will be liberated from its bondage to decay and brought into the glorious freedom of the children of God. We know that the whole creation has been groaning as in the pains of childbirth right up to the present time. Not only so, but we ourselves, who have the first fruits of the Spirit, groan inwardly as we wait eagerly for adoption as sons, the redemption of our bodies.' (*Romans* 8 v 19 and 21-23)

Before I finish this chapter I should comment briefly on miracles.

The so called 'Deist' belief is that God created the universe with its natural laws and then let it continue under its own steam. This is the kind of theology which would fit best with an old fashioned Newtonian view of the universe as governed by rigid fixed laws of nature contained within an absolute space and time. It would be a deterministic universe in which every event would be completely predictable in accordance with fixed laws of nature. It would be a closed universe with, in principle, no way of interacting with anything beyond it. Thus a continuing dynamic relationship between God and nature would be impossible without upsetting the basis of creation itself. Miracles would be inconceivable in such a universe.

However, as we have seen, this is not the universe which is disclosing itself to science. We have to do with a universe of nature which is very much open and non-deterministic, dependent for its continuing being on God.

Christians believe that God has bound Himself to creaturely existence by the incarnation of His Eternal Son, in whom we are able to call His Father, our Father. In His life, death and resurrection He renews a world that has been spoilt by man's misuse of freedom. It is in the light of this that we must understand the miracles of the Bible and the Church as being part of the renewal of all things in Christ.

I believe that as we discover the fundamental structure of life, we shall find that it too is open to a Word of Life from beyond. How sad that many 'theologians' and bishops reject miracles including the Virgin Birth and Bodily Resurrection of Christ. They are deluded by an out of date science and needlessly do harm to the faith of millions.

3. LIFE

It is very difficult to define what life is. However, we all know that there is a very obvious distinction between things that are alive (such as people, dogs, ants, roses and bacteria) and things that are not alive (such as stones, air, water, cars and computers). It is also clear that we human beings cannot manufacture life out of 'dead' matter. Put all the scientists in the world together and they will never be able to make a single blade of grass (except from other grasses). This fact in itself should cause us a great deal of thought. Why can they not make living things? It is probably true that 'life' involves a dimension of reality which is beyond the scope of our four dimensional world of space-time and therefore beyond complete scientific definition. However, there is also a much more obvious reason, from within nature itself, as to why life seems so hard to produce and that is its sheer complexity – way, way beyond the complexity of anything ever made by mankind.

We all tend to take life for granted because it is all around us. Billions of blades of grass grow and wither every year. The hairs on our head grow, are cut, and then are discarded several times each year. Why should Jesus say that the hairs on our head are all numbered by God? Aren't they really very insignificant? It may seem so, but each living hair is far more complex and amazing than any machine or computer built by man. We rightly gasp with amazement when we see the computer technology necessary to send human beings into space, but we have lost our sense of awe at the greater complexity of even the simplest form of life. When Jesus spoke of the lilies of the field and said that not even Solomon in all his glory was arrayed as one of these, some of his listeners may have thought he was exaggerating. But He wasn't. Indeed it is one of the greatest understatements in the whole Bible. The more the botanist's learning penetrates into the lilies of the field, the more complexity, wonder, mystery and beauty he finds. This is not only true of flowers but of all life, including the very simplest single cell of life – the bacterium. Gone is the day when the amoeba was thought to be a relatively uncomplex form of life. The even more 'simple' bacterium is more complex than a complex chemical factory, correctly connected to a very complex computer, and all contained within a fraction of a cubic millimetre.

We really should not be surprised at such discoveries. Should it not be obvious to us that the mere fact that we cannot manufacture life, must mean that its complexity is far greater than anything we have yet made? To many, the thought of a 'God' making the universe, seems too incredible. Granted, such a belief is amazing, but then we are surrounded by an amazing world, so then *any* explanation will seem incredible. However, we must learn to separate explanations which can be shown to be nonsense and go *contrary* to the observed facts, from that one which not only fits the facts but liberates the mind to explore the wonders of nature even more. I believe, the theory that life as we see it today evolved by mere chance processes, not only is contradicted by hard evidence, not only is a complete nonsense, but inhibits the thinking of scientists and slows down the advance of knowledge. Fred Hoyle, the great astronomer (not a Christian believer), says that in succeeding generations it will be asked why the theory of evolution, now so eloquently propounded by many, was ever believed. The answer, he says, will not be that it was believed for scientific reasons, but sociological reasons. By this I take it to mean that evolution as a mechanistic explanation for the genesis and development of life was believed because of peer pressure amongst scientists to maintain the theory. To drop the theory of evolution would cause such huge upsets in how we *like* to view the world that its demise would seem unbearable to many. Hence the peer pressure. If scientists think they are immune from peer pressure then let them look at the history of science!

However, this does not mean I am merely adopting the position of the so called 'scientific creationists'. These are the people (often reputable scientists in their own fields) who hold to a view of Genesis 1, that the universe was created in a literal six times twenty four hour period, approximately ten thousand years ago. Nor does it mean that I deny all evolutionary processes in nature. I need to expand on what my position is. The scientific creationists are really making two points and it is a pity that these two points are often confused in debate.

Firstly, they are claiming that mechanistic evolution cannot be the explanation for the origins of the species of life as we see them today. With this I agree. The case I believe is overwhelming. Secondly, some of them claim that the earth and the universe are relatively young (a mere 10,000 years old) compared with the scientific establishment's belief that the universe is thousands of millions of years old. On this point I am far from sure. There are indeed things in nature that point to a young universe (thickness of the dust layer on the moon, for example), but there are also many other things that point to a very old universe (the sheer size of the universe and time taken for light to travel from distant galaxies, for example). The time taken for the supposed evolutionary processes to produce life as we see it today is not a valid argument because this is precisely one of the main points at issue. (Yet the time framework for evolution was used as a yardstick for dating strata in rocks. This was quite wrong.)

More fundamentally, the scientific creationists, and some of their opponents, are operating with a Newtonian view of time as an eternal absolute. As we saw in Chapter 1, time is not an eternal container for events but part of nature itself. It, too, was created out of nothing. Relativity theory teaches us that light is a more fundamental constituent of the universe than even time. This is also implied in the opening verses of Genesis 1. To apply our time frames to the early 'days' of creation is therefore mistaken.

As I said above, it is a pity that these two issues (Is mechanistic evolution an explanation for the origin of the species of life? and, How old is the universe?) get confused in the debate. If one reads the evolutionists' arguments against the scientific creationists, one finds that their arguments for an old universe have real substance, but their arguments attacking the anti-evolution position of the creationists amount to little more than insult, in which they call their opponents obscurantists etc. These intimidatory insults are a cover for no argument at all. The argument that, of course all enlightened people believe in evolution, really will not do.

I did once believe in evolution, for after all everyone believes it to be true. Any visitor to a Natural History Museum or listener to a David Attenborough programme on the television will testify to that. I assumed that God had used the supposed mechanistic evolutionary processes to produce life as we have it today, so that we human beings are not only descended from the ancestors of monkeys, but also from jelly fish too. I was then a theistic evolutionist. I believed in evolution and in God. The two, as it were, had worked together to produce human beings. Many Christians still hold this position today. One can, if one uses one's imagination, easily fit evolution into Genesis 1. All one has to say is that the Hebrew word for day can mean a very long time and there you have it – Genesis 1 and evolution in harmony. This seems even more convincing because the *order* of creation of life in Genesis 1 (fish, birds, reptiles, mammals, human beings) is the same as the evolutionary theory supposes. (An interesting point in itself.) But this is not really a Biblical evidence for evolution, but only an observation that the Biblical record tallies with the *fossil record* of the rocks, which is a different though remarkable fact.

The fact that many Christians do believe in evolution is evidence that Christian believers can be open minded. God could have created the main species separately or He could have used evolution to do it. Atheists and people who do not want God involved in their origins *cannot* be open minded. They are forced to believe in evolution, whatever the facts of scientific discovery may produce. They may admit that there are many problems with the theory of evolution, but they can never abandon it because they have ruled God out from the beginning. However, I am not ruling out some form of evolutionary change in nature.

When Charles Darwin visited the Galapagos Islands of the Pacific Ocean he found that the same animal, or bird, had significant variations from one island to another island. What is more, these variations helped the particular species of animal, or bird, to survive in the differing features of the islands. This was particularly true of the giant tortoise and the finch.

Not only was it true of birds and animals, but also of plants, such as the prickly pear cactus. On relatively dry islands, where the main food for the giant tortoise is a tall cactus, the tortoises are found to have long necks. The tortoises that are found on wet islands, where grass is the main food, have short necks, suitable for eating vegetation at ground level. Charles Darwin believed that these variations had been brought about by natural selection. We all know that within one species of animal there are many variations. Darwin believed that those variations which were less suitable to the environment would not survive well and therefore would not produce similar offspring, so that eventually only those variations most suitable to the environment would survive in a particular geographical location. This is what seems to have happened on the Galapagos Islands.

It seems common sense and is what is often called 'survival of the fittest' or 'natural selection'. This kind of evolution does seem to take place and is often called *micro* evolution. It does not involve an increase in complexity but only a modulation in the complexity of an animal or plant.

It gives no explanation as to how one animal or plant can change into another. It does not explain how creatures without bones will develop bones, how creatures with cold blood will become warm blooded, how creatures without eyes and ears will develop eyes and ears. An organ, like an eye, is such a fantastic complex interdependent *whole* that a gradual change from no sight at all to a seeing eye seems ridiculous. There are many varieties of dogs that have evolved from one another, but they are still dogs and can breed with one another as dogs. This is micro evolution. Dogs, however, do not change into reptiles, cats, birds or fish however much time and changing circumstances they are given. If all the land was flooded, dogs would not gradually change to fish – they would drown! Natural selection cannot explain an *increase* in complexity.

A popular view of evolutionary changes goes back to Lamarck who preceded Darwin. Although discredited in the scientific world a long time ago, it is still assumed to be true by many lay people. It is the view that the characteristics we acquire during our life can be passed on to our children in a hereditary process. So a seven stone weakling who works hard to develop into a muscular he-man will pass on his acquired characteristic of physical strength to his children in his genes.

It is this kind of theory that is popularly believed to have produced the giraffe. A horse like animal has to reach even higher and higher for its food, stretching its neck more and more and giving birth to offspring with long necks. This however is not true.

Our inherited characteristics do not depend upon the characteristics that our parents have acquired during their lifetime by dieting or exercising. Our inherited characteristics are dependent upon an extremely complex computer programme contained in our genes, which is derived from both our parents. They cannot alter the programme they will pass on to us by their eating and behavioural habits during their life. Lamarck's theory of evolution is therefore wrong.

Lamarck didn't know about this computer programme which exists in all of life. This computer programme is the extremely complex and highly ordered DNA molecule which makes up the nucleus of every cell of life from bacterium, plant, animal, to human being. I believe that the discovery of DNA makes Darwin's theory even more impossible to accept and demonstrates more than anything else the incredible complexity of life. Each form of life has a different DNA programme which determines whether it will develop into a grass, animal or human. Each human being has a different programme which determines the colour of his eyes and all his other physical characteristics. This is true for all species of life. What then does cause change (mutation) in the computer programme passed on from one generation to another? The present orthodoxy among biologists and botanists is that changes are purely random, caused by accidental copying errors from one generation to another. However, these random changes are extremely rare (the DNA is very good at copying itself) and when the changes do occur they are not beneficial, but almost always harmful or lethal. Changes in the DNA do take place more frequently when life comes under the influence of outside interferences such as chemicals or radiation. Some biologists have postulated that the apparent sudden appearance of new species in the fossil record has been caused by periods of abnormal amounts of cosmic radiation penetrating the earth's atmosphere and impinging upon life. It is true that if such radiation did reach the surface of the earth it would cause random changes in the DNA structure of life. *But* this would be harmful, not beneficial in its effect. We all know that when parents are accidentally exposed to radiation (as at Hiroshima or Chernobyl) there is not a great expectancy that future generations of humans will be born with marvellous improvements (e.g. wings with feathers to enable them to fly) but a terrible fear that babies will be born with deformities, missing limbs and brain damage.

Of course copying errors of the DNA do occur. There is approximately one chance in ten million that they will occur in one life cycle. Of these mutations, one in 1,000 will be non harmful or beneficial. So as one animal produces its offspring, there will be one in ten thousand million chances of a non harmful mutation. Given a very, very large population of a particular species, it would be expected that non harmful mutations will occur from time to time and these will be spread throughout the species in succeeding generations. If these non harmful mutations prove beneficial they will by the process of the survival of the fittest or natural selection, become established in the species. It is these differences within a species that enable a mating pair to produce offspring with their own unique properties. (No two human beings are completely indentical except for identical twins who do share the same DNA pattern.)

However, for a completely new structure to develop, (such as a limb or an organ), many beneficial changes would be required to take place *simultaneously*. The possibility of this happening by chance even once in the life of the universe is effectively zero.

At the beginning of this year (1987) a television programme was produced called *The Blind Watchmaker*, which tried to show that evolutionary changes could take place by chance. The presenter of the programme had programmed a computer which would show how certain creatures could develop new limbs. The following week, in the Letter's Page of the Radio Times, someone pointed out that this only worked because he had pre-programmed the computer. Who, the correspondent asked, programmed nature's computer in the beginning? The presenter of the programme responded by saying that there wasn't enough space to answer the point. The truth is, there is no answer, and millions of viewers have been hoodwinked, yet again, by a man who will not think straight.

Ah, but some may say, although we do not yet know mechanisms that produce beneficial changes in the DNA, is it not possible that succeeding generations of scientists may discover these mechanisms? To this I respond with a question.

Why should we believe in mechanistic evolution as the reason for the origin of species? As we have seen above, there is no possible mechanism of evolution known to us that would produce these changes, so is there any hard evidence in the history of this planet that one species has developed into another species? The only hard facts we have about the history of life on this planet are the fossil records. What do they show?

Contrary to what many popular books about origins of life say, there are comparatively few places in the world where the strata of the rocks have not been upset by geological movements. Only where there has been relative stability in the rocks, over supposed millions of years, can we get a good perspective on the history of life from the fossil record. Where there is relative stability, we find a little evidence for micro-evolution (small changes within a species, without an increase in complexity), but no evidence for gradual changes, giving birth to entirely new species. On the contrary, the fossil record shows the marvellous stability of species over millions of years. (We now know this is due to the stability of the DNA.) This marvellous stability is punctuated by *sudden* appearances of many new species, whilst many of the older species continue in existence relatively unchanged. The gradual change from one species to another is simply not in the fossil record. The fossil record provides no evidence for *macro*-evolution, but it is the kind of record we would expect if the main species of life were created separately by God. It would also correspond to seemingly spontaneous changes in the DNA if the DNA were open to a Principle of Life beyond it. Would this be what the Scripture calls the Logos or Word of Life? Darwin admitted that the fossil record did not back his theory but expected that future discoveries in the rock strata would prove him right. In fact the reverse has happened.

I began this section by saying that all the scientists in the world cannot make a single blade of grass and one of the reasons for this is the sheer complexity of life. However, one of the basic constituents of life can be made in the laboratory. Electric sparks, passed through hydrogen and ammonia, can produce the relatively simple amino acids. Amino acids are not life, but are necessary for the formation of life. There are many different kinds of amino acids and if they are arranged together in a highly complex and precise order they make a protein. What are the chances of them coming together in precisely the right order? Fred Hoyle (*The Intelligent Universe* – page 12) estimates that it would take 100 × the age of the universe, to produce just one protein by chance and yet we use 200,000 types of proteins in our cells. Some biologists speak of amino acids swimming around in the early oceans of this world and finding suitable partners to make up the protein. But they cannot say how amino acids (which are not alive and have no intelligence) know which of their fellow amino acids they must join with, in precisely the correct sequence, to form a protein.

In laboratory tests it is possible to encourage amino acids to form the right chain, but only by adding an enzyme (a type of protein) to the mixture. So we need a protein to make a protein! How is that for a theory which tries to explain the origin of proteins? So how are proteins made in nature? They are manufactured from the amino acids by a process using the DNA computer programme which we have already referred to. So we think we have the answer! But all we have done is push the problem one stage further back and instead of simplifying it we have made it more difficult, for the DNA is much, much more complex than the protein; and how in the world did the DNA manufacture itself? When I was a boy, man-made computers were as large as large buildings. Through wonderful progress in technology and science we can make the same computer the size of a typewriter or even a watch. Which is more wonderful, the small or the large? The small, of course. Can one imagine earthquakes, wind and fires in the world accidentally assembling a large computer, even if they did shake, blow and burn for millions and billions of years? No. They wouldn't even build a house! They might build several caves, but that would be it. So how did the random events of our early earth produce a computer more complex than any man made computer, and contain it within a fraction of a cubic millimetre?

But that is what we are led to believe actually happened! How man hates to believe in God! How he loves to be totally self-sufficient!

Nature's little DNA computer is the minimum requirement for any life at all. It is the centre of the nucleus of a single cell of the bacterium. Round the nucleus is the cytoplasm which is a highly complex chemical factory in which proteins are manufactured. The DNA at the centre sends messages to the cytoplasm using the RNA intermediary which copies and translates the language into messages that can be received by the cytoplasm. So the *simplest* form of life contains at least three main ingredients – a highly complex computer, a highly complex chemical factory and a highly complex communication system – and all three must be connected to one another correctly for life to exist in its very simplest form.

We may think that the difference between a boneless, sightless jelly fish and a human being (containing bones, eyes, ears, liver, kidneys, lungs and brain) is very large; but it is not as large as the step from no life to the simplest cell of life, which is still less complex than a jelly fish!

There is an interesting comment by a mathematician Douglas R. Hofstradter in his brilliant book *Gödel, Escher, Bach – An Eternal Golden Braid.* It certainly is not a Christian or religious book but on page 54 he says:

> 'A natural and fundamental question to ask, on learning of these incredibly, intricately interlocking pieces of software and hardware is: "How did they ever get started in the first place?" It is truly a baffling thing. One has to imagine some sort of bootstrap process occurring, somewhat like that which is used in the development of new computer languages – but a bootstrap from simple molecules to entire cells is almost beyond one's power to imagine. There are various theories on the origin of life. They all run aground on this most central of all central questions: "How did the Genetic Code, along with the mechanisms for its translation originate?" For the moment we will have to content ourselves with a sense of wonder and awe, rather than with an answer.'

Just one more point (which I owe to Prof. E. J. Ambrose) about the complexity of the human body. In our brains there are 500 million neurons (brain cells). Each cell is able to make thousands of connections. Each neuron is like a telephone exchange connected by wires to thousands of houses. The brain is like 500 million telephone exchanges (not mere telephones, but telephone exchanges). The connections possible are $10^{1,300,000,000,000}$ and these must be connected in the right way! We cannot imagine a number like that. The number of atoms in all the galaxies of the whole universe is probably less than 10^{72} and the number of seconds since the big bang is less than a mere 10^{18}. How anyone with a brain can believe that the human brain is the result of mere chance processes is beyond me! What a wonderful and awesome thing it is to be a human being, and yet how stupid can we be! Would a monkey be so daft?

The most popular belief about the theory of evolution is that we humans are descended from monkeys. Actually most evolutionists say that humans and monkeys have a common ancestor. Although the fossil record does not show this, one thing is said to back it up, namely that certain types of monkey have a very similar DNA code to a human code. There is only a few per cent difference between the two codes. Does this not show that we must have had a common ancestor?

It sounds plausible, but is it? My Ford Sierra has a great deal in common with its larger 'brother' the Ford Granada. Does this mean that the Ford Granada is descended from the Sierra or does it not rather show that they both have the same maker? Monkeys and men may have a lot in common. It doesn't mean they are descended from a common ancestor but similarities would be expected if they had the same Maker!

At the beginning of this chapter I said life is difficult to define. A wonderful thing about life is its flow. As a boy I lived near the river Thames in Middlesex, England. Last year I revisited my old haunts by the river. The river was the same river, yet the millions of molecules that had flowed past me as a child were long gone and probably would never return to the river. If the flow of the river had been stopped by a huge dam to keep the old water in, it would soon have become stagnant. The life of the river was its flow and the river was the same river because its *pattern* of flow made by its banks had remained the same. It is the same with life. The cells of life containing the DNA and the cytoplasm are not static machines. Rather, new molecules continue to flow in and then out of the cell so although it is ever being renewed it retains its pattern. When the flow stops the cell is dead. On a larger scale, the cells themselves come and then go from the total organism of our bodies. Every few years we can say that the cells we had a few years ago are now all gone and replaced by new ones. Yet I am still me! The pattern is the same. If the flow stops, my body will be dead. So the substance of my body is not the real me, no more than the individual molecules of the river are the river. My life is the pattern. If that pattern is preserved and renewed when the substance of my body is destroyed, then I still live and am not dead at all. Is this a little of what the Bible means by the resurrection of the body? Anthony Flew (atheist and joint editor of the book New Essays in Philosophical Theology) fails to understand this point. In an article on Death he pours scorn on the notion of life after death by assuming that the real 'me' is merely the molecules of which I am made. Life with its flow is far more wonderful than he has ever imagined.

Professor E. J. Ambrose is surely right in saying that without a belief in the after life our understanding of the biological world is incomplete.

The Bible speaks of the source of the order in the world as the Holy Spirit. It was the Holy Spirit who moved over the primeval waters of the earth and brought life into being. It is man's rejection of God's Spirit which has caused the world to gradually decay into disorder. It is the same Holy Spirit who is the power of the resurrection of Jesus – the beginning of the renewal of all things. It is the Apostle Paul who speaks of the power that enables Christ to bring everything under control – that same power that will transform our lowly bodies so that they will be like His glorious body (*Philippians*,3 v 20 and 21).

4. THE SCEPTICAL PHILOSOPHERS

Many people reading the previous chapters will think that my arguments are just really an updated version of the old arguments for the existence of God. The philosophers of old looked at the wonderful structure of nature and said there must be a Divine cause, or Divine designer who made it all. Yes, my points are in principle similar to theirs. But have not more modern materialistic philosophers, onward from David Hume, demolished these arguments with their persistent logic? Certainly their arguments did have a great deal of force in their time. However, even if the Christian cannot immediately think of a reply to them, he or she must not be too quickly dismayed. If the philospher's conclusions go against our deep intuitive common sense then *they*, not *we*, are probably wrong and will be shown to be so by succeeding generations of philosophers.

Much of the arguments of the past are about whether or not the universe was *designed*, by a *Designer*. This implies a view of God as a great Architect and Craftsman. I do not deny this view of God's creative work, but prefer to speak of Him as calling into existence and being the universe of nature in harmony (not identity) with His own Being and Beauty. However, for the sake of this Chapter, I will use the term 'design' to describe God's creative work.

William Paley (1743-1805) appealed to our intuitive common sense. He imagined a traveller walking in the desert coming across a rock. If he asks himself how its shape came to be, he can reasonably assume it is as it is because of the chance processes of wind, heat and cold that have acted upon it. If the traveller comes across a watch (a pre-quartz model) he will notice that it contains cogs, wheels, and springs all very carefully put together in a complex machine so as to accurately measure the passage of time. If the traveller asks himself how the watch came to be as it is, he will not conclude that its parts were all accidently assembled by the chance processes of wind, heat and cold but will assume that it was made by an intelligent designer and craftsman. Who could disagree with him? If the traveller then considers the world with its teeming life, he will notice that it too is like a complex mechanism so it too must have been made by an intelligent craftsman and designer, who is God. Isn't Paley simply appealing to our ordinary intuitive common sense? Yes he is, and I agree with him. However, many clever philosophers have attempted to show his argument is false. Before I tackle their arguments, I want to make my own position clear.

I am not wanting to revive a form of so called 'natural theology'. In the middle ages some theologians of the church believed that our knowledge of God was given in two parts. Firstly, we could know certain things about God using our natural reason. That is to say, we could develop part of our theology simply by applying our reason to the wonders of nature. Our theology would then be made complete by adding on to our natural theology, that which God revealed to us in Christ, the Bible and the Church, which we would receive, not by natural reason, but by faith. So our knowledge of God would derive partly from reason (natural theology) and partly from faith (revealed theology). I do not accept this.

I believe that the *whole* of our knowledge of God comes to us in faith and repentance, if we humbly open our lives to His Word and Spirit. The way of knowing God is then entirely by faith, not natural reason. *However*, nature with all its wonder does prompt us to seek God in faith. Nature does leave us without excuse, if we refuse to seek God. We do not discover God in nature, but nature does point us to that which is beyond it – that which we cannot know at all without humble faith and repentance.

Any book on the philosophy of Religion will refer to the 13th Century Catholic theologian Thomas Aquinas, who expounded five ways we can know there is a God. Four of these ways really belong together as one way explained from four different view points. First, we see things moving, so there must have been something that moved first to begin the chain of movement that we observe. This first mover is God. Secondly, we see in nature that nothing happens without a cause, so there must have been a first cause that set the chain of cause and effect going. This first cause is God. Thirdly, everything that exists depends on something else (that is to say, everything in nature is contingent), so that there must be a being on whom everything is ultimately dependent and He Himself not being dependent on anything. That being is God. Fourthly, nature fits in beautifully with itself. It is a highly complex interdependent whole, so it must have been designed by a designer and that designer is God.

Thomas Aquinas did see a difficulty with the first three of these arguments. What if the series of cause and effect were infinite – would not that mean there is no need to postulate a first cause? (This difficulty assumes an infinite universe without any beginning – a very outdated assumption). Modern followers of Thomas Aquinus have argued that even if there was an infinite series of causes and effects then this series would still be dependent on a reality beyond it.

I considered the possibility of their being an infinite series of cause and effect in the chapter on quantum physics. Let me re-cap. We explain the behaviour of a substance by the molecules from which it is made. But why do the molecules behave as they do? We can explain this by the atoms from which they are made. But why do atoms behave as they do? We can explain this by considering the properties of the protons, neutrons and electrons from which they are made. And so on, for ever! Either we will never be out of work delving even deeper into the subatomic wave particles and therefore never finally being able to explain the natural laws of physics *or* we will reach the fundamental building blocks of mass/energy but not know why they behave as they do, there being nothing more basic from which to explain them. It seems to me that we are probably at the second alternative because quantum physics teaches us that, in principle, the behaviour of electrons, quarks (quarks are the building blocks of protons and neutrons), and their inter connecting wave particles cannot be predicted merely from within nature. In the quantum world there are effects without natural causes. This points to the belief that electrons etc., are fundamental and their behaviour depends on a reality beyond nature. So whether or not the series is infinite, it must still be dependent on what is beyond it.

Before we move on to consider the sceptical philosophers who argue against Aquinas and Paley, I want to say something about a 20th Century extreme form of scepticism which was first known as Logical Positivism.

Briefly, it invented what is called the Verification Principle which states that any statement that cannot be verified or falsified by sense experience, is meaningless. Since statements about God are not (it is said) verified or falsified in this way, they are meaningless. The problem with this philosophy is that it is self contradictory. The Verification Principle itself is a statement which cannot be verified or falsified by sense experience and therefore by its own definition is meaningless. So the whole of the philosophy of logical positivism collapses in ruins before it begins and this is generally recognised today. It is an example of what I said above, that if the clever arguments of the philosophers contradict common sense and intuition, they will probably be shown to be wrong by the next generation of philosophers. The reason for mentioning this philosophy here is that it did have a great impact on Western 20th Century thought – an impact from which our social sciences have still not recovered. Although a complete nonsense, it was an attractive philosophy for the atheist because he could wriggle out of serious discussions about the existence of God by simply saying all such discussions are meaningless. How easily can even intelligent people be blinded! The less 'learned' may or may not agree with the statement that God exists, but they surely know it is not a meaningless statement and they are, of course, right.

Now let us consider the sceptical philosophers who argue against Aquinas and Paley. The greatest such philosopher was David Hume, already referred to. Although he wrote before William Paley, he does attack very similar arguments to Paley's argument, from design. The sceptical philosophers, since David Hume, have added little to his basic arguments – they have just rehashed them and attempted to update them. David Hume's most readable (and indeed entertaining) arguments are found in his *Dialogues Concerning Natural Religion*. He invents a character, Cleanthes, who is a very good exponent of the argument from design, for the existence of God. However, Cleanthes is outdone by another fictional character. He is the sceptic, Philo, who probably represents the views of David Hume himself. (There is a third character, Demea, but he is not relevant to my basic argument.)

We will consider David Hume's points.

1. He says the universe is bound to have the *appearance* of design. Any universe would need to have its parts adapted to one another. That is to say; any universe would have to have some order. Since we know any universe would *appear* to be designed, how do we know that *the* universe *is designed?*

In one of his other works, in which he discusses analogical reasoning, he makes a related point. For simplicity I will quote John Hick's summary of his argument in *Philosophy of Religion*, page 29:

> 'The fact that there is only one universe precludes our making probable judgements about it. If – impossibly – we knew that there were a number of universes (e.g. 10) and if in addition we knew that (say) half of these were God-produced and half not, then we would deduce that the probability of our own universe being God-produced would be one in two. However, since by the universe we mean the totality of all that is (other than the creator of the universe), clearly no reasoning based on frequency theory of probability is possible concerning its character.'

The false assumption behind this reasoning is the belief that it is possible to have a *non* designed universe. In fact, it is not possible. Any universe would appear to be designed because there can be no natural existence without design, whatever form it takes.

Order, as we have said many times, is not self generating. This is the second law of thermodynamics. Relatively minor adaptions can take place by themselves (e.g. in micro-evolution) but they do not mean an increase in information content or complexity in the real sense. Existence involves a tremendous amount of order, even if we are only talking about the existence of a single atom. The existence of anything means its parts must hold together and relate to one another and they cannot do this unless there are fundamental laws of existence which presuppose order. Any natural existence would appear ordered because any natural existence would *be* ordered. Another hypothetical universe might have completely different laws of nature than ours but it would still have to have some laws of nature, and therefore would have been designed by a Designer.

Related to this point, John Hick (*Philosophy of Religion*, page 21) asks, 'How do we know that the universe is not a mere unintelligible brute fact?' Well, if it were, science would be impossible. This question shows that John Hick doesn't understand the necessary relationship between existence and order. One cannot have one without the other.

2. David Hume rejects this argument from order by saying that in an infinite space of time all the atoms of the universe will randomly arrange themselves in every conceivable combination so that the present arrangement of life on planet earth was bound to occur sometime. Bertrand Russell also used this argument. It is like the argument that, given sufficient time, a monkey just randomly hitting the keys of a typewriter, would type out the Encyclopaedia Britannica. This is one of those arguments which one instinctively feels is wrong, but it is difficult to show what is wrong with it. Well, in the first place, if orthodox science is correct, the universe is not infinite in duration (a mere 15,000 million years, which is probably not long enough for a monkey to randomly type out the first two sentences of Britannica). Secondly, physics and common sense recognise the existence of order. As we have noted, the second law of thermodynamics teaches us, that unless the Universe is open to a Mind beyond it a local increase in order will result in an overall increase in disorder. The incredible local order required to randomly produce the Encyclopaedia would mean that a corresponding increase in total disorder in the universe would overwhelm and destroy the monkey and the typewriter long before the encyclopaedia was complete. Fred Hoyle (*The Intelligent Universe*, page 11) puts it in a more picturesque way by saying that the whole universe would not be able to contain the wastepaper baskets necessary to receive the rubbish that the monkey had typed out before it accidentally typed out the encyclopaedia. What is more, the order, information and meaning in the encyclopaedia is minuscule compared with the information content of the natural order as revealed by modern physics and biology.

(For the sake of argument, let us say a monkey took at least one million years to accidentally type the first sentence of the encyclopaedia – not an unreasonable assumption. How long would it take to accidentally type the first two sentences, one after the other? The answer is not a million plus a million, but a million times a million years, or about eighty times the life of the universe and that only for two sentences of the encyclopaedia in correct sequence. Remember too, the information content of nature is far far far greater than the information content of all the encyclopaedias of the world put together.)

So now what do we think of David Hume's argument that given enough time the atoms of the universe will randomly produce life on earth? The real fault with the argument is that it assumes that all combinations of atoms are equally stable. But a highly ordered structure is less stable than a pile of rubbish. I can illustrate this by considering two piles of bricks. One pile is just a random jumble of bricks and the other is a highly ordered structure of bricks which are made into a building. The first is stable, the second is unstable. An earthquake applied to the first pile may move the bricks around, but will not alter what it is, namely a jumble of bricks. An earthquake applied to the second will destroy the building, and will never accidentally re-assemble it. So order is unstable and disorder is stable. That is why the atoms of the universe, even given an infinite span of time, can never arrange themselves in the highly ordered way necessary to produce life.

3. David Hume challenges the analogy between the order of nature and the order of a machine. He says, why not compare the world of nature with an animal, or a mind, rather than a machine like a watch. A watch is made by a craftsman, but an animal comes into existence by the process of conception and birth. A mind has its own order within itself.

It is true that the world of nature is not simply a machine like a very complicated watch. Nevertheless it is *at least* a machine. Minds and animals have not always existed. The whole process of the formation of animals and minds from one generation to another is a mechanism. It is more than a mechanism but it is still a mechanism. The universe is 'machine plus'.

4. David Hume rightly says that if the order of nature were created by a Supreme Being, then He must have order in Himself. He then asks, 'If a Supreme Being is capable of having non contingent order, why should not the world have a non-created order?' This is another way of asking, 'Who made God?' This question is based on a category mistake. It applies a principle of nature – namely, that effects have causes – to the realm of the supernatural. The question as to who made something, is a question only applicable to the something if it is part of the natural order. We cannot know from nature what questions are applicable to that which is beyond nature. What we know is that order in nature cannot be completely self existent or self explanatory. This is not only a consequence of Gödel's theorem, it is common sense.

There is an interesting essay in the book *New Essays in Philosophical Theology*, edited by Flew & McIntyre. The essay is by J. J. C. Smart. In it he uses all the arguments of David Hume to attack William Paley's argument from design. He is completely convinced of the success of his arguments, but right at the end of his sceptical essay, he makes an interesting confession. Referring to the cosmological and design arguments for the existence of God, he says:

> 'However, now let us ask, "Why should anything exist at all?" Logic seems to tell us that the only answer which is not absurd is to say, "Why shouldn't it?" Nevertheless, though I know how any answer on the lines of the cosmological argument can be pulled to pieces by a correct logic, I still feel I want to go on asking the question. Indeed, though logic has taught me to look at such a question with the gravest suspicion, my mind often seems to reel under the immense significance it has for me. That anything should exist at all does seem to me a matter of the deepest awe.'

The reason for this paradox in J. J. C. Smart's thinking is that in his deepest being he feels his own sceptical logic is not in tune with reality. His sense of awe is not irrational. It bears witness to the existence of a logic deeper than he has yet discovered. Yes, the wonders of nature not only bear witness to the reality of God, but they also fill us with awe.

The writer of Psalm 77 notes how the wonders of creation bear witness to the power of the Creator, but then he goes further and says, 'Your ways, O God, are holy'. If you or I have ever experienced awe before a sunset or flower or the stars, we know we cannot at that same moment be thinking evil. Nature bears witness not only to the power of God but also to His holiness!

So why is there evil in the world? Why does God not remove it? This is the question philosophers, including David Hume, have asked down the ages. If God is both all powerful and all good, why does He not remove evil now? Here I must make several points.

1. Christian teaching is that God really did give man both freedom and power over the world. We really do have the power to influence ourselves and nature for good or evil. It is not God who is the author of evil.

2. It will be asked, what about suffering, caused by nature – earthquakes, poisonous snakes, disease etc. Surely we cannot blame these on mankind? Well, firstly, the Bible does speak of the whole of nature groaning in travail until man is set free from sin. Secondly, quantum physics is pointing to a far far more profound interaction between man and the very fabric of nature than we have ever imagined before. This may seem to be far fetched, but it is worth noting. If our human consciousness affects the nature of the electron with which we are interacting, then the very foundation of the natural order is influenced by human sin. This is still a deep mystery.

3. God *has* come to deal with sin. In His great love, He has borne the sin and suffering of the world throughout history. In all our affliction He too is afflicted. The great sign and climax of this is the Cross of Jesus, on which He died for our sins. He now gives us time to turn back to Him before He comes to destroy all evil at the end of the age.

4. If He were to destroy all evil now, He would have to destroy us because we all have a share in the sin of the world.

It is precisely because God *is* love that He delays the coming of His Kingdom. Do we really want His Kingdom to come? Would we be ready to face Him? First, as Jesus said, the Gospel of the Kingdom must be preached in all the world, as testimony to all nations, and then the end will come!

David Hume makes another point and with this I agree. He says nature does not of itself lead to the God of the Bible. Even if we acknowledge a creation, how do we know *from nature* that it was an *infinite* God? How do we know it was a perfect God? How do we know it was one God, rather than a committee of gods?

Nature, I acknowledge, is not the *way* of knowing God. As we have said, it does leave us without excuse for not seeking God, but it isn't the way we know Him. We'll return to this point in a minute.

There is, though, I believe, a remarkable testimony to the truth of the Christian Bible, that is found in the history of the world. The subject of almost all of the Old Testament, and much of the New Testament, is the unique relationship between God and the people of Israel – the Jews. The history of the Jews is indeed unique and awesome, as many commentators (Christians, Jews and agnostics) have noticed.

I quote a passage from Lance Lambert's book *The Uniqueness of Israel*, page 57 and 58:

> 'In 1899, Mark Twain wrote an essay which he entitled *Concerning the Jews*, and brought it to a remarkable conclusion. We must remember that this was long before the Balfour Declaration of 1917, let alone the re-creation of the State of Israel in 1948. He wrote:
>
> "If the statistics are right, the Jews constitute but 0.1 per cent of the human race. It suggests a nebulous dim puff of star dust lost in the blaze of the Milky Way. Properly the Jew ought hardly to be heard of; but he is heard of, has always been heard of. He is as prominent on the planet as any other people, and his commercial importance is extravagantly out of proportion to the smallness of his bulk. His contributions to the world's list of great names in literature, science, art, music, finance, medicine and abstruse learning are also way out of proportion to the weakness of his numbers. He has made a marvellous fight in this world, in all the ages; and has done it with his hands tied behind him. He could be vain of himself, and be excused for it. The Egyptian, the Babylonian and the Persian rose, filled the planet with sound and spendour, then faded to dream-stuff and passed away; the Greek and the Roman followed, and made a vast noise, and they are gone; other peoples have sprung up and held their torch high for a time, but it burned out, and they sit in twilight now, or have vanished. The Jew saw them all, beat them all, and is now what he always was, exhibiting no decadence, no

infirmities of age, no weakening of his parts, no slowing of his energies, no dulling of his alert and aggressive mind. All things are mortal but the Jew; all other forces pass, but he remains. What is the secret of his immortality?"

At the same time Leo Tolstoy wrote an essay in a similar vein which he entitled *What is a Jew?*. In it he wrote:

"This question is not at all so odd as it seems. Let us see what peculiar kind of creature the Jew is, which all the rulers and all the nations have together and separately abused and molested, oppressed and persecuted, trampled and butchered, burned and hanged, and, in spite of all this, is yet alive ... the Jew is the emblem of eternity. He whom neither slaughter nor torture of himself for years could destroy; he whom neither fire nor sword, nor inquisition was able to wipe from off the face of the earth; he who was the first to produce the oracles of God; he who has been for so long a time the guardian of prophecy, and who has transmitted it to the rest of the world – such a nation cannot be destroyed. The Jew is everlasting as eternity itself."

There can be only one answer to Mark Twain's question, 'What is the secret of his immortality?'. The secret of the Jewish immortality is God himself. In the book of Malachi God declares: 'For I the Lord change not; therefore ye, O sons of Jacob, are not consumed.' (*Malachi* 3 v 6 R.V.)'

Not only is their history different, it fulfils Biblical Prophecy in remarkable ways, and has a very deep significance for the meaning of the way of salvation for all mankind. For a fuller exposition of this, see my small book 'World Hope in the Middle East', published by Handsel Press.

. . . .

At the beginning of this chapter I spoke of the way of knowing God as humble faith and repentance. That is to say, our knowledge of God involves ourselves at a very deep level. Both subject and object are involved in knowledge of God.

This is true of all knowledge. All true scientific enquiry must involve an openness to new truth on the part of the scientist. He must allow the object he is studying to disclose itself to him as he is willing to 'repent' of pre-conceived notions. This is particularly true in relativity theory and in quantum physics. In relativity theory the relationship of velocity between the observer (the subject) and the thing observed (the object) affects the whole time and space reference of the measurements made. In quantum theory the scientist's own consciousness is bound up with the measurements he makes of the quanta.

Similarly, in our knowledge of God, if we do not wish Him actually to impinge upon our lives, challenging our intellectual, moral and spiritual being, then we will never know Him and in a terrible sense He will not know us. Jesus told us of those terrible words that would be spoken to many on the final day when we all give an account of ourselves to Him. 'I never knew you, depart from me ...' By His grace and mercy, may these words never be said to those who read this. Simple faith and repentance will open a door into a whole new universe of knowledge. The Word we hear, though deep in its challenge to our lives, will be a Word of Life, Hope and Love.

BIBLIOGRAPHY

DAVIES, Paul: *God and the New Physics.*
POLKINGHORNE, John: *One World.*
HOYLE, Fred: *The Intelligent Universe.*
AMBROSE, E. J.: *The Nature and Origin of the Biological World.*
WEINBERG, Steven: *The First Three Minutes.*
LAMBERT, Lance: *The Uniqueness of Israel.*
HICK, John: *Philosophy of Religion.*
HUME, David: *Dialogues Concerning Natural Religion.*
FLEW, Anthony and MCINTYRE, Alasdair: *New Essays in Philosophical Theology.*
TAYLOR, Howard: *World Hope in the Middle East.*
PRIGOGINE, Ilya and STENGERS, Isabella: *Order out of Chaos.*
TORRANCE, D. W. (Ed.): *The Witness of the Jews to God.* (especially the article *The Destiny and Vocation of Israel* by TORRANCE, T. F.)
HOFSTADTER, Douglas R.: *Gödel, Escher, Bach; An Eternal Golden Braid.*